# TAIWAN
*An Underrated Paradise*

*Diary of a Traveling Black Woman: A Guide to International Travel*

*Mini Travel Guide Series*

*Dubai, Abu Dhabi & The 5 Other Emirates You Didn't Know About*

*Jamaica: Likkle, but Tallawah!*

*Studying Abroad for Black Women*

*Iceland: Nature, Nurture, & Adventure*

*Solo Travel: Try It At Least Once!*

*Trinidad: ...More than Just Carnival*

*And more...*

Diary of a Traveling Black Woman:
A Guide to International Travel

"Mini Travel Guide Series"
Volume X - Taiwan

# Taiwan:
# An Underrated Paradise

Brittany Edwards

**The Traveling Black Women Network**
Grace Royal International, LLC
Atlanta, GA

The intent of the author is to offer general information on travel to
Taiwan. The author assumes no responsibility for the actions of the
reader.

Cover Model: Brittany Edwards
Cover Design: Nadine C. Duncan
Interior Design: Nadine C. Duncan

ISBN: 979-8-9862680-2-6
ISBN: 979-8-9862680-3-3 (eBook)

2nd Edition, June 2022
Travel Guide Series, Volume X
Printed in the United States of America

Published in the United States by:
Traveling Black Women™
Grace Royal International, LLC
Atlanta, GA 30316

www.travelingblackwomen.com

For my countless friends and family who encouraged me to dream.

Special appreciation to Anika Ullah, Fulbright Research Scholar and National Geographic Explorer, for her insight to the nuances of betel nut in Taiwan.

# Contents

somewhere above the clouds

January 2019

# Preface

Taiwan is complicated. It is urban overgrown with leaves and oversized trees tipping off balconies. It is the formless hues of deep sunset skies shaped by the architecture of cascading tea terraces and magic in the ordinary lives of people, full of hospitality. Traditional characters in modern settings occasionally read from right to left, but mostly left to right, sometimes top to bottom. Mountains challenge the bounds of sky, reaching through her clouds. Betel nut trees replace skyscrapers. Taiwan is a lawless place. Watermelon insides are yellow and guava's are white. Pomegranates grow wild at the temple across the street from my home. Gorges threaten to split the earth to its very core as waterfalls flow nearby. And in a cave on the outskirts of a mountain fire lives harmoniously with water. Taiwan is the co-existence of paradox— bustling and still, known and chartless, enchanting and ordinary.

"Anyone who visits Taiwan, loves Taiwan," they asserted. And it seems I've entered an inextricable chasm, falling endlessly in love with Taiwan over and over again— in love with the abandoned train tracks turned bike trails through the caverns of mountains or bridges from which to watch the sunsets that I've chased here more than anywhere else, in love with fruits whose sweetness defy the very existence of sugar, in love with the periwinkle silhouettes of mountains layered bewitchingly against the sky. Rubber bands stretch diagonally end to end, securing the lid of a wax box or spin around the mouth of a plastic bag sloshing with noodles. A metal crane disturbs stuffed animals, clawing at their resting place. The hot air, winding roads, and luscious elevation remind me of my parent's home in Jamaica. Taiwan is home. Taiwan is me. Merging identities to form a melting pot of a personality. Blending old with new. Traditional culture with 21st century. It is cinnamon and star anise, mangoes and sugar cane.

I was transplanted with blindfolded roots,

deconstructing and constructing my identity colored by the curious composition of prejudice and admiration, as many felt fear and awe from the depth of my skin, and clouded with confusion as I tried to navigate the miscomprehension of my existence warped in the curiosity and questioning of remote communities. Frustration chaperoned my inability to communicate with the limbs of logic and reasoning severed from my vocabulary. But in the absence of that identity, I rediscovered another part of myself.

Sometimes, I felt the weight of my Blackness beyond their eyes and into the unspoken responsibility I bore as a representative for my people around the world. And sometimes I feared the impression left, wasn't a favorable one. Returning warmth and smiles to cold staring eyes would be exhausting, as would reciprocating connection with every eye. It would drain my energy granting attention to so many, all the time. So I kept my head up and eyes straight, walking with confidence and defiance. I felt empowered to make eye contact to curtail staring. But still remained that worry that I, with eyebrows furrowed partially because of the sun and partially from annoyance, did not always come across friendly.

Eyes might linger on the darkness of your

skin or pierce through the woven pattern of your hair, but here I've seen my Blackness offer privilege. It was jarring. Suddenly the identity my society seasoned with distaste for dark skin created disappeared in the mouths of another culture. As I glared at the shopkeeper tracking me through the store, I realized it was not due to fearing me a thief, but fearing as a foreigner I would need help finding an item. There are no threats here. It's absolutely liberating.

Maybe it's confusion, but it looks more like distaste when some see me. Not all the time. Not even a majority of the time. But in the rural areas, it happens enough. I see them in the reflection of storefronts, through tinted car windows, and scooter side view mirrors. But sometimes when they see me, it's like they've seen Christmas morning.

"Woah!" I hear a small voice exhale. I look to see the cutest girl enamored with my melanin. As I smile and wave, she waves her yellow fan and her little hand. When her family notices, they wave furiously and shout,"HELLO!… HELLO!… NICE TO MEET YOU!!!!" I chuckle and continue walking. Complicated.

We take the short cut through the temple across the street, but run into an elderly lady that lives nearby with a small congregation of neighbors. She was an English teacher, so conversation flows easy. "Out by the temple is cooler than inside the house," she comments. It is. I thought she meant cool as in cool, but I realize she's using cool for colder. "Where are you going?" Out for dinner. "So late? Wait, wait, wait, we'll bring you some food." She calls to a younger man and he rides off on his scooter returning with steamed buns stuffed with braised meat, and fried octopus balls, and spring rolls and the food keeps coming. As other neighbors come through, food is pushed into their hands and they stop to eat.

Touched by the tenderness of a people, I curiously began unraveling an elaborate web detailing the foundation of their contemporary society and culture that latently instills a set of ethics and values increasingly scare in our world plagued by the race to the bottom— a system of social mobility whereby socio-economic deregulation exploits resources and people, ultimately compromising the public good for increased economic activity.

• • •

In my peripheral I glimpse hasty cameras capturing blurred imagery of who I am forgetting that what I am is human— just with skin a little darker, hair coiled more tightly—, a human who feels the stab of every lens, flash, snap, click, gnawing at my skin as the mindless preservation of things consumes their consciousness. It's changed the way I travel.

Writing became my way of taking photos, of capturing moments in their space and time because I'm often grieving how precious memories are as they're being made. And I try to hold on to them. And I'm trying to hold on to less things— less pictures, less preserving. And I'm trying to just live in balance and flow and letting go.

So I've stopped holding moments captive, opting to relish in the evanescence of memories. And the moments, I've found, mean more when you appreciate their transience and your fortune to live them, right now. Above all else, I've kept the reminder that these are people living ordinary lives in normal places. We tend to forget that.

# What to Know

歴史 | *History*
*lìk - sú*

"*Have you heard of* White Terror?" he almost secretly asks as if someone might hear beyond the sealed windows and into the white Toyota Camry. Although he was only two at the time, friends and family filled his memory with stories. Gesturing towards the central island as we enter the roundabout, he explains executions happened there. My eyebrows pinch as I glance around, looking for some indication of a memorial site. Yet the cheery sun and unextraordinary junction spoke of no time when individuals were imprisoned and massacred for their perceived or real opposition to the Chinese Nationalist Party (KMT, Kuomintang) when the political group fled to Taiwan after defeat in the Chinese Civil War. Chiang Kai-shek targeted intellectual minds and social elites fearing their resistance to rule or sympathy with Chinese communism, resulting in a period of martial law from 1949 to 1987 known as White Terror. The sound of genocidal gunshots ending just 33 years ago still silently echo off the walls of sunken alleyway as it remains a sensitive and unmentioned blemish of Taiwan's history.

Even so, the people radiate the same warmth as the island's sun. Formosa. Beautiful island. The Republic of Formosa existed from the 23rd of May in 1895 until the Japanese occupation of Taiwan in October later that year. Taiwan was ceded to Japan by China under the Treaty of Shimonoseki during the First Sino-Japanese War and Taiwanese notables resisted with a proclamation declaring the democratic Republic of Formosa.

The Japanese would not have any part of it. They occupied Taiwan and with relative speed defeated the Formosan resistance. This commenced five decades of Japanese rule, where Taiwanese culture and religion were outlawed to encourage firm assimilation to the Japanese Empire. During World War II, the return of Taiwan would be included in the Allies' war aims—four years before Chiang Kai-shek would  arrive, toting White Terror along. Today Taiwan is democratically lead by female President Tsai-Ingwen as a Republic of China.

# What's the relationship between Taiwan and China now?

The tension is almost indiscernible because it's one of those conversations left mute. But it definitely exists. "If China ever invades Taiwan, remember me," he says half jokingly but unease shifts in his eyes as his gaze returns to the half-lifted chopsticks over a bowl of rice and he continues eating. It's silent. Like the echo of White Terror. And my dear friend entreats that it's better to live in peace under the suzerainty of China than to stir catastrophe. Again.

Violence is missing from Taiwan. It's a place where cat calls can land a man in jail and cultural expectations of honor coupled with social pressure creates an order that constituents dare not challenge. Arriving from the United States, I found the peace and security of Taiwan perplexing. As I struggled explaining to my students that "i" before "e" except after "c" isn't always true or shrugged my shoulders when they ask why nasty and tasty are pronounced differently, I began critically examining my language and their own. Turning over the society in my mind I wondered whether their peace rooted in the pragmatism of their language. There are no nonsensical words. No exceptions to rules. It's always "i" before "e" except after "c". Teaching my confused students that sometimes in English the rules don't apply left me thinking about how language rules with exceptions might paint mutable boundaries around ethics within societies. But in Taiwan, there are rules, and they are followed. Herein lies my exploration of the intricacies that define relationships to understand what ramifications the interplay between language and ethics has for the global community. Could it be that the inconsistency within the English language latently instills the belief that rules are not always meant to be followed? Is a culture of defiance and recklessness reinforced? What is the role of linguistic relativism in creating a peaceful society?

In Taiwan, language has become a device for neocolonialism. Mandarin Chinese and English have navigated to the forefront of linguistic preferences as the main languages used to communicate in the metropolises, causing the sixteen officially recognized aboriginal languages to slip from public ear. But the further inland you travel, the more you will connect with societies that operate almost exclusively in a different tongue. Stepping into the fresh produce and hanging meat of the farmer's market, Hokkien, common-

ly called Taiwanese, flies back and forth between vendors. My mandarin is of no use here.

It's the older generations. Some students, even immersed in these communities, know only a sprinkle of their ancestors' speech as Mandarin is the language they study in, play with their friends in, and order food in. How do you preserve one culture when washed over by another? Responsibility has fallen into the hands of elders to convince posterity their culture matters.

*Atayal youth at Thanksgiving celebration*
*November 2018*

• • •

We form a circle, hand in hand, one foot crossing in front of the other moving counter clockwise, in a cheerful cadence tempting time to reverse to the simplicity of aboriginal life before ore mining brought bulldozed communities and explosions into the heart of their land.

Bamboo tubes filled with sticky rice explode against the pavement as we strike it open and a prideful Atayal smile saunters my way toting a crate with something special he insists on sharing with me. The Thanksgiving feast is full of light-hearted jest, dancing, and traditional meals. He sets a piece of honeycomb on my plate, so fresh my eyes lock on the bee wing I'm eating as chunks of the carcasses remain mixed into the honey.

Tucked in the mountains of Taichung county, bright red textiles woven with horizontal black stripes and trims of yellow and green adorn the inked skin of the Atayal aboriginal people. The facial tattoos used to indicate distinctions within the social hierarchy and differentiate between ethnicities was a significant rite of passage necessary between the ages of five and fifteen. Girls who have proven their weaving dexterity earn hers while boys must prove their worth to the tribe through hunting or headhunting.

Elders describe the pain of traditional inking methods as worse than death itself— an integral part of the ritual to signify one's strength to endure anything. Now the ritual practice meets resistance with the younger generations' preference for adapting to the times and seamlessly integrating with Taiwan's greater society. In the final months of 2019, 97 year old Lawa Piheg passed, taking the last of these traditional face tattoos with her.

• • •

Suddenly I was flying through the air, mounting a horse with no warning and no saddle. "Just hold on to the mane," he reassures as I worry the burrs at the hem of my pants might hurt Tornado. We waded through the manicured park's overgrown brush until a clearing where a loose tether allows Tornado to roam. That weekend we spent with a member of the Paiwan indigenous community, lovingly referred to as Boss.

The Paiwan mostly live in Pingtung and Taitung counties. Female chiefs and female shamans head their matriarchal society; status within their hierarchal social structure is inherited at birth. They use the Five-Year Festival as a cultural and historical mechanism of distinguishing themselves, re-connecting, and uniting with their ethnic group.

.

• • •

Amis red is muted by neon pinks, yellows, and greens. Headdresses adorned with fur, feathers, poufs and sometimes artificial flowers are trimmed with a beaded fringe. Multilayered fabrics, braided segments and beads hang loosely around the necks of the largest ethnic group among Taiwanese aboriginals. Song and dance rise from drums beating throughout the community as infectious sounds of the Harvest Festival ring in the Amis New Year. Their struggles have bred a generation of singer-activists empowered by cultural rediscovery hoping to preserve and revitalize their language by learning traditional songs from elders and transposing them into this space and time.

Forty traditional instruments mingle to create a harmony reflecting their social system that balances power between men and woman equitably, stemming from its matriarchal roots. Music has become a means of tending to the psychological and historical trauma wounds centuries of discrimination and indoctrinated inferiority created. It's a coping mechanism for colonialism bringing land loss and thereby destroying the relationship they cherished with their land, their people, and the Spirit. When the KMT arrived, they effectively claimed eminent domain over the majority of the island, mining for ore in sacred places. Of the 174 mines in Taiwan 105 are on indigenous land.

With each wave of settlers, the aboriginal populations were pushed deeper towards the the belly of the island, up into the mountains. During the Japanese occupation and assimilation period, cultural tools and artifacts were confiscated and destroyed. It's a familiar story—indigenous people forced from the lands called home and relocated to new places by strangers. Now, they struggle to maintain their rights. As they are tucked in remote areas, access to resources like education and healthcare are remedial. This causes a pressured emigration into the city, pulling them further way from their heritage.

Aboriginal settlements were pushed to the foot of mountains with the risk mudslides and earthquakes would once again wipe away the serenity they've made home. Our way of life is fixed to culture. Losing the traditional ways of family rearing, causes the integrity of the community to collapse. This is the song of all aboriginal voices.

The enculturation of ethnic groups has made delineating the sixteen officially recognized boundaries— Amis, Atayal, Paiwan, Bunun, Puyuma, Rukai, Tsou, Saisiyat, Yami (the Taos), Thao, Kavalan, Truku, Kizaya, Seediq, Hla'alua and Kanakanavu— difficult. They make up only two percent of Taiwan's total population with their rich culture further diluted by the lure of assimilating to the popular norms of today. As aborigines make their way to cities, ethnic mainstreaming rises in response. Ethnic mainstreaming is the spirit of human rights protection, promoting the sustainable development of harmony between ethnic groups. It aims to raise familiarity and awareness for civil servants regarding the cultural and ethnic diversity of indigenous peoples; it aims to deepen compassion.

As public servants learn how to approach difficulties faced by various ethnic groups, they are fostering the distinctive identities and subjectivities to accept the independent and equal identity of each population. Ultimately, their aim is to create an environment that encourages autonomous thriving as groups sustainably grow together. When the government staff understands, accepts and adapts to the differences inherent in the cultures of these peoples, they can implement policy that is proactive in mitigating the encountered problems.

In the more agrarian communities, you might notice crimson-stained teeth or splotches on the pavement and spitting from scooters. This is betel nut. This is why ethnic mainstreaming matters. Flashing luminescent signs directing customers to vendors called "betel nut beauties" has darkened the rapport of a traditionally venerated plant. This fruit of the Areca Palm, commonly found in Oceanic societies, has garnered an uncouth reputation by the Han-Chinese descent majority in Taiwan who have come to view it as an addictive stimulant that poses a severe health hazard. While betel nut contains naturally occurring cancerous compounds, the commodification of this crop during China's colonization encouraged the addition of unregulated pesticides that would come to exacerbate the naturally present elements and cause Taiwan to develop the highest incidence of oral cancer in the world.

      The tall and slender palm decorating the terrain of Taiwan stretches beyond the stereotypes that its fruit is uncivilized and dangerous, reaching into the rich core of environmental sustainability for indigenous peoples. Its hardy trunk ensures structural integrity within traditional architecture, fallen fronds are harvested and transformed into plates, sandals, card holders, and contemporary art by laser incisions. For the indigenous, this versatile plant is nature's gift. The round shape of betel nut is a symbol of fertility, while its growth in bunches signifies abundance. It holds deep meaning in weddings, rituals, and between lovers: a man must bring a branch to the home of his betrothed; the leaf cradles a betel nut, cigarettes and bamboo cup of rice wine in offering as prayers ask ancestors for their blessing; the small gift unites. It is key in life ceremonies and used with intention. It was decontextualized.

The plant was twisted into a cash crop marketed towards laborers of demanding occupations for the rush or high that accompanies chewing betel quid. So now, legislators must comprehend how to delicately balance a health care dilemma and cultural preservation. How do we ensure pieces of a culture are approached with sensitivity to prevent erosion?

Language is trying to remain ashore. You'll hear public transportation announcements in four languages: Mandarin, Taiwanese, Hakka, and English. But, the Taiwanese and aboriginal language has been similarly marginalized. It is slowly disappearing, suffocated by Mandarin. Mandarin Chinese is the national language spoken in Taiwan. You'll find mostly the older population speaking Taiwanese, especially those in the greener countryside. Taiwan's indigenous languages are slipping from the Earth's surface; languages a number of international experts identify as the origin of the Austronesian culture.

This is the abbreviated story of an island with towering cliffsides crashing into the cerulean Pacific Ocean— a history, bitter and sweet like its fruits, complicated like its terrain, and a little stinky like its tofu.

*T*aiwan allows 60 countries to visit without a visa. With a United States passport, your roundtrip ticket grants you a 90-day all-access pass to the island. As for vaccines, there's nothing out of the ordinary. So you'll be on your way to Taiwan in no time! More likely than not, the main "Taipei" TPE airport will be your arrival destination through one of the major international airlines to Taiwan, EVA Air (Star Alliance) or China Airlines (SkyTeam). I was scandalized to find out the airport wasn't exactly in Taipei, but actually its neighboring county, Taoyuan. The airport physically in Taipei is Taipei Songshan Airport (TSA) but that's only helpful to consider if you are arriving to Taiwan from another part of Asia. You can also consider Kaohsiung (KHH) on the southern tip or Taichung (RMQ) on the west.

Flying into Taoyuan isn't much of an inconvenience because Taiwan is blessed to have the high speed train running along the island's west coast. From Taoyuan to Taipei, it's a quick 15 minute ride for NT$160, just about $US6—and from one end of Taiwan to the other, the total commute time on the high speed train is just over 1.5 hours.

Something that shook me to the core of my foundation while making my departure from Taiwan back to the United States was finding out that I could check my luggage into my flight from Taipei Main Station train terminal. At the area to take the high speed train to Taoyuan airport, you can check your luggage directly onto your airline's carrier to lighten your 15-minute commute. Note that you can only do this a maximum of two hours before your flight.

• • •

It's a modest society. Wearing the girls out and short shorts will garner more eyes staring in your direction, but they easily recognize foreigners and understand that non-locals accord themselves differently. I'd still recommend dressing on the more family friendly side of the spectrum. Women wear long loose fitting clothes—and bras. You might come across the mini-skirt culture, but they're hardly worn by anyone under the age of 30. The youth of Taiwan don't hold back on their fashion, so feel confidant to go all out in whatever it is you like, because their couture is not monolithic. But it's rare to see athleisure there.

Oh yea, it's also a "one-piece" society. Again, they recognize that foreigners do things outside of their local norms, so you can get away with wearing a two-piece swimsuit. You'll just attract a lot more attention. And a monokini is pushing it. To be honest, a majority of women there are wearing something like a rash guard. If you wear a two piece, I'd recommend doing so with company rather than solo.

If you're coming from North America, you don't need to worry about packing any wall adapters because Taiwan shares the same outlet and electrical standard, 110V/60 Hz AC.

• • •

Put your plastic away because cash rules in Taiwan. While there are some establishments that will run credit or debit cards, they are not commonly found. Especially not in the markets. You're safer using your debit or credit cards in a place that looks like your traditional brick and mortar. But even that can't be trusted. Just carry around cash. You always have the option of with-drawing funds at a convenience store ATM, but you might find better rates at the airport kiosks. FYI: the New Taiwan Dollar (NT$) is sometimes noted as TWD.

• • •

      Gift giving culture is huge. If you're visiting with any locals, I recommend packing a small gift for them. It doesn't need to be anything fancy or large; it can literally be chocolate (just not Ferrero Rocher or Snickers or anything too regular that they might be able to find in Taiwan), it can be a key chain or a magnet. Just pack something about the country you're from and they will love it. This is an especially considerate thing to do if you're staying at a homestay as the host will really appreciate the small gesture and might feel even more invested in you as a guest. This thoughtfulness opens the chance of building a deeper relationship with a local. And that's invaluable.

# 住所 | *Accommodations*

*tsŭ-sòo*

*This is the travel hack* of a lifetime. Motels. American motels and Taiwanese motels are two completely different things— but they do share an infamous reputation. Motels in Taiwan are absolute luxury, but they're a taboo concept because it's a "hotel for lovers." Once you get over the concept that it has a reputation for scandalous activity and accept that people will engage in scandalous activities regardless of whether or not a hotel is marketed for such (and don't freak out about the unconventional toiletry offerings) you'll allow yourself to live your best travel life. For the approximate cost of a "regular" hotel in America— when I say regular I'm meaning the amenities they offer— you'll relax in a 1 bedroom suite with a private elevator, mini fridge with complimentary snacks, private balcony, 6 person jacuzzi hot tub with ceiling water stream, shower room with wall jets and a dry sauna. All en-suite. It's really cute. All for USD$70 per night. Oh and I almost forgot to mention, a respectful complimentary breakfast is served in the morning.

If the bells and whistles are not for you, there are also a number of hostels to meet just about every traveler's need. For the extra introvert, there are capsule hotels. About USD$10 a night rents you your own private space ship. Ok, it's not actually a space ship but you almost couldn't tell. Taiwan is a hostel society, which is fabulous for traveling. A hostel is a communal room with individual beds. Your bed space ranges in privacy— from no curtain to closing door. There are many different themed hostels to cater to different personalities and help diversify their business from the others. That's where the capsule hotel comes in.

Glowing blue lights illuminate your bunker equipped with everything you need— private air cooling controls, a tv, and outlets. If you're claustrophobic maybe sit this one out. Also, don't let the low price fool you. The place is not lacking in quality, with plenty of new amenities.

Dragon & Tiger pagodas at Lotus Lake in Kaohsiung

September 2018

言語 | *Language*

*giǎn -gí*

*This is a section for* those who want to challenge themselves to engage with the language during their trip. I would encourage you to try speaking it even once or twice with a local as they will light up, thrilled that you have even tried. It might allow for a beautiful connection with someone. You really don't need to worry about memorizing anything or speaking the language perfectly because it is common for people to know English in brick and mortar spaces. At the farmers market you're more likely to run into an older individual who has no hold on the English language, but they might have a young person with their stall who they'll ask to flex their English muscles.

If you already know Madarin, you might face a different obstacle. I noticed a lot of people suffer from "skin deafness." They're deaf when they see your skin is not like theirs. Since they automatically assume you don't know the language, they stop listening to what you say. I'll ask a question or order my food in Mandarin and they go to call someone else who speaks English. Then we speak in Mandarin with each other. Sometimes they'll speak in English and I'll answer in Mandarin. And sometimes we'll have a complex conversation about the nuisances of my meal and they'll write down the price because they think I won't understand basic numbers. But it's not just a 'me' experience. It's a frustrating linguistic phenomenon where people believe that they cannot understand you and simply choose not to listen.

## *The Basics...*

早
*zǎo*

Morning

早安
*zǎo ān*

Good Morning

你好
*nǐ hǎo*

Hello

拜拜
*bàibāi*

Bye Bye (informal)

再見
*zàijiàn*

Goodbye (formal)

謝謝
*xièxiè*

Thank you

## *Shopping*

廁所在哪裡？
*cèsuǒ zài nǎlǐ*

Where is the bathroom?

加熱嗎
*jiārè ma*

Heat it up?

這個是多少？
*zhège shì duōshǎo*

How much is this?

可以便宜一點嗎？
*kěyǐ piányí yìdiǎn ma*

Can it be a little cheaper?

沒有
*méiyǒu*

Don't have

不用
*búyòng*

Don't need

Many people in Taiwan are familiar with very basic English, especially if they are in a customer facing role. In the cases where you are experiencing a language gap, it's important to use simple terms. Instead of "Can I use your restroom?" you can just ask, "Toilet?" And it's better to just say "Hot," instead of "Can you please heat it up?" Just remember to add your "thank you's" to sound like you've had good home training.

Often times if you're shopping in a chain store, the cashier may ask if you have a loyalty card, which you can reply *méiyǒu* and then whether or not you'd like a bag. It will be a variation of "*dàizi yào ma?*" or "*yào dàizi ma?*" That's when you'll see "*bùyòng*" come in. Alternatively you can always just say "no."

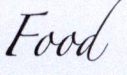

*Food*

## The savory things you'll want to try:

螺肉飯                                     Braised Pork Rice
*luó ròu fàn*

| | |
|---|---|
| 湯包 or 小籠包<br>*tāng bāo / xiǎo lóng bāo* | Soup Dumplings |
| 雞排<br>*jī pái* | Chicken Fillet |
| 蛋餅<br>*dàn bǐng* | Egg Pancake |
| 牛肉麵<br>*niúròu miàn* | Beef Noodle Soup |

## The desserts you'll want to try:

| | |
|---|---|
| 湯圓<br>*tāngyuán* | Rice Balls |
| 芒果奶雪花冰<br>*mángguō nǎi xuěhuā bīng* | Mango Milk Snowflake Ice |

## Foods for the adventurous:

| | |
|---|---|
| 臭豆腐<br>*chòu dòufu* | Stinky Tofu |

皮蛋
*pídàn*

Thousand Year Old Egg

豬血糕
*zhū xiě gāo*

Pig Blood Cake

## Souvenir snacks:

牛轧糖
*Niú gá táng*

Nougat

牛轧糖
*Fènglí sū*

Pineapple Cake

太陽餅
*Tàiyáng bǐng*

Sun Cake

## How to order tea:

一杯
*yìbēi*

One Cup

熱的
*rè de*

Hot

| 冰的<br>*bīng de* | Cold |
| 半糖<br>*bàn táng* | Half Sweet |
| 微糖<br>*wēi táng* | Little Sweet |
| 無糖<br>*wú táng* | Sugar Free |
| 珍珠<br>*zhēnzhū* | Boba |

My favorite "tea" is *dōngguā* (冬瓜，winter melon). It's a dynamic fruit that when unripe is used as a vegetable similar to chayote. Winter Melon technically doesn't count as tea, but is a great caffeine-free beverage that you'll find frequently on the menu. If you want to step it up a notch try the Winter Melon milk with boba. Another delicious topping (that's actually on the bottom) for your tea is herbal grass jelly. Now be mindful, this herbal and marginally sweet topping isn't for everyone, but it is culturally common. It's best paired with an Assam or Oolong tea.

If you're thinking, "This is great, but how can I be sure I'm pronouncing everything correctly?" scan the QR code to access multimedia supplements that will help you better prepare for your trip! There you will find links to audio-visuals that facilitate language practice, my favorite accommodations, the online booking system for the Alishan Forrest Railway, and more! Taiwan is quite simply the love of my life and I could speak its beauty ad nauseam. Even within these one hundred pages, I feel as though we'll just scratch the surface of all Taiwan has to offer.

scan me

Or search @brittany-edwards on Medium.com
for the article "Taiwan: An Underrated Paradise"

# What to Expect

# *Being a Black Woman*

*O*ne thing *I* recommend is joining the Brothas and Sistas of Taiwan Facebook page right before your trip to see if there are any impending meet ups or events where you can connect with expats. Or maybe you'll just want to grab coffee and get some more local insight on the ground. There is a growing community of Black expats in Asia, so keep this advice in mind for any travel on that side of the globe.

• • •

I crossed the rainy street to meet brown skin and a smile standing under an umbrella. She tells me that she saw me across the street and turned back, waiting for me to cross. We embrace, walk and talk, then say our goodbyes. "Brittany, was that your friend?" No, I have no idea who that was. It's just the camaraderie of our community.

Let's be real. It's a homogenous culture. That makes it very hard to conceptualize the ex- istence of people who look like us. The closer to the big cities you stay, the less you'll realize, but travel towards the belly of Taiwan and you'll feel increased stares, conversations, and photos. The paparazzi treatment is not nearly severe as the one I experienced in China, but there was one extreme incident.

The two men dressed all in black make me feel uncomfortable the first moment I see them as I leave the grocery store. I drop only the bananas in my basket and continue walking to the fruit stand. I'm back at my bike and he comes over to me, peels back the plastic, and peers at the contents of my bag. "Tasty," he says. Yup. The discomfort grows. The other one suggests he and I take a picture. I don't want to. But he insists. So I turn my head down and focus on leaving. He forces his way around my bike, between the pillar and next to me. I'm repeating I don't want to, I don't want to, I don't want to. The wind carries his faint smell of alcohol at 3:30 on a Sunday afternoon. Click. I'm fumbling as the passion fruit drops out of my basket and the heavy bag of groceries hanging on the handle threatens to topple the whole bike over. Click. He's taking photos. Click. Finally it's the sound of my lock releasing. But they've already gotten what they wanted. I feel upset, powerless, and violated as I ride away.

They're curious. To see someone like me somewhere like there, in Changhua county, is golden. Their knowledge of the Black diaspora is effectively non-existent. In their society where the majority of people are of the same or similar race and ethnicity, it's hard for them to cognitively engage with the existence of a diverse nation. Black is Africa. A merchant in the market confidently greets me with a "Namaste." It takes me another "Namaste" and a confused brow to realize that she thought I was from India.

Clicking through the TV channels in our cabin, we land on Save the Last Dance. As the three of us snuggle under heated blankets, we're gawking at how bizarre this is. How is this niche movie actually playing on the television in our cabin on this remote tea farm in the middle of Taiwan? Is this really the version of Blackness that they're exposed to? Is there anything that's not from the turn of the century?

There

Dancers pay homage to Japanese influence
November 2018

is colorism in Taiwan. Their standard of beauty is white. Yet deep shades run through some of their skin. Taiwan is varied in the way its people look. Dark skin is equated to lower class, working outside perhaps in the farming industry while light skin is equated to wealth status— you know your typical complexion complex. You'll need to be wary of skin products there because many will have bleaching agents euphemistically advertised as brightening or lightening. You'll be surprised to see how many dark skin Asians there are, because they remain so well hidden from media.

But even though their standard of beauty is white, I receive compliments. Sometimes to my face, and sometimes as an impulsive exasperation. Beautiful. So cute. "You have such beautiful eyes," she repeats. I thought her English was flawed. It's not often a brown girl gets complimented on her brown eyes. We're only taught that lighter colors make eyes beautiful. And my eyes, plain brown, have no decoration, no shadow, no mascara, and sit below brows that I've let connect. It's like their standards of beauty apply to themselves and not to outsiders.

I was living in a surreal world where Black skin gives you special treatment. The *āyí* at the front is so excited to see me and infatuated with my Chinese (my outfit was pretty cute, too) so she hurriedly brings me to the *lǎobǎn* who runs the shop. They felt different. There was this genuine sweetness to their excitement. He suggests, "Let's take a photo!" We head over to the kiln where they shot part of the Netflix documentary, in the fifth episode of Asia Street Food. Uncle Goats' fame stems from unearthing and revitalizing a traditional recipe that he risks his life to create. A mixture of Chinese medicinal herbs, eleven full bottles of rice wine and chunks of goat are added to an earthenware pot which is then covered with foil and caked with mud before burying for three days in a smokey walk-in oven of burning rice and millet husks that heat the stew to a temperature of one thousand degrees.

Neither my phone nor Chinese are really set up that way, so I did not call to make a reservation. I just showed up early and hoped for the best. This isn't the type of place you should show up to without a reservation. Yet somehow, she put me in a private room with air conditioning; the *lǎobǎn* announced my presence to the crowd as if I were some distinguished guest and called me to the front of the line welcoming me as the first to enter the cooking chamber.

• • •

"Hey! This is Santa from the Netherlands"she exclaims as she excitedly brings a package near. But I can't focus on the plastic Santa, because my eyes immediately focus in on the two figurines next to him. *Blackface*. And I try to keep a pleasant face while I debate whether or not I should point out what those "genies" actually are and why they're so problematic. "And they say to the children that if you are naughty, the genies will take you away to Spain." And I think, maybe that is why some children feel scared and cry when they see me.

It doesn't seem easy for them to conceptualize racism, cultural appropriation, and why these things are problematic, because not only does it not concern them personally, it is not a major part of the direct world around them. Their homogenous environment seems to breed a naiveté that softens a need to engage with other truths. In all of this, remember they are homogenous, but not a monolith.

# The Trip

*I*f for some reason you can't head immediately to your accommodation, know that they have storage lockers all around Taipei Main Station that you can leave your bags in for a couple of hours while exploring the city. You know, they say the best way to beat your jet lag is to fight the urge to sleep and stay awake until Taiwan's darkness settles, but to each their own. Two things to note about storing baggage. One is that the lockers are almost all always full. I managed to stumble across one practically empty area— it was in a less popular location. You'll find a plethora of lockers as you're exiting the facility and making your way above ground. You'll even see them on wings of the shopping complex. Most of them are on the smaller side and cannot fit a standard full size check on luggage, but the offered locker sizes do vary.

The down side to these is that you have no idea what is available in the area until you arrive. To avoid this you can book a Lalalocker. With this company you can pre-check available lockers in an area, book it and then proceed as usual. They have a flat rate of NT$150 (Around US$5) for large luggage and smaller pieces come in at NT$70 (Around US$2.50). It's a part of the share economy so lockers can be found anywhere from restaurants to stores and hotels.

I recommend leaving your locker somewhere above ground because it's a little bit easier to have visual cues that remind you of the location rather than trying to find your way back down and through the overwhelming maze that is Taipei Main Station. That building is so utterly confusing. If you ever need to meet someone there, just please do both of yourselves a favor and do not meet inside Taipei Main Station. You'll thank me later.

## Transportation

First things first: it's illegal to eat or drink on public transit— yes, even water— and as a result order and cleanliness abound. Floor markings indicate waiting lines for alighting train passengers. Silence settles in the train cars and buses for the duration of your commute. It's unreal. They are always so silent. Our group attracted a lot of eyes and attention, not because we looked different, but because the volume we carried was relatively loud. I don't think Taiwanese people are accustomed to laughing. Not the bellyaching laughter that seizes control over your entire body. Not the deep laughs where you just can't stop laughing and maybe a tear or two rolls out of your eyes. I did see people laugh and joke, but never that deeply.

Now that that's communicated, you need to know there are a handful of public transit options. Taiwan High Speed Rail (THSR/HSR) is different from the Taiwan Railway Administration (TRA). The TRA is the local train. And then in big cities like Taipei and Kaohsiung, you can find the Mass Rapid Transit (MRT) system; Taichung should have one up and running soon. To be honest, the TRA and MRT are pretty similar except the TRA is above ground and not nearly as fancy as the MRT.

More than once, I found myself taking a 7 mile bike ride home not on my own will but because the buses in my county stop running at 8pm. Thankfully not all of Taiwan is like Changhua. In addition to the local buses, there's a Taiwan Tourist Shuttle in Taipei coordinated with the tourism bureau to make destinations like Alishan, Kenting, and Taitung more accessible. They also typically have English markings, making them more convenient.

To this day, I'm unsure whether it's an EC card or an "EasyCard," but this is your public transit pass. Tap at turnstiles to enter train platforms or upon bus embarkation. EasyCards can be purchased at MRT stations or convenience stores like 7-eleven and Family Mart. It's also simple to add value to your EasyCard at convenience stores. Just mention to the teller you'd like to *jiā zhí* (價值) and mention how much. They'll ask you to put your card on the EasyCard platform and then work some magic.

Remember that lawlessness I mentioned? There's an inconsistent protocol: in big cities, you only tap once, however in smaller urban areas, you might need to tap on and off with your EasyCard on busses. You'll hear each stop announced in four languages: first Mandarin, then Taiwanese, Hakka, and finally English.

I can understand if public transit is not your thing, or the anxiety of approaching that unfamiliar system is high. If you don't feel comfortable hailing down a taxi and communicating where you need to go, you can always ask your hotel to call one for you. Remember when you're leaving to take a business card from your accommodation so you can show it to a driver on your way back. To be honest, someone might even ask you for your business card. Business card culture is very much alive and thriving in Taiwan. Ok, we're getting distracted... A taxi will be the most expensive mode of transportation, but it's not ridiculous. The base rate where the meter starts is somewhere around NT$80, so just under USD$3 and ticks up in increments of NT$5 based on time and distance. Although it's a scooter society, all of the taxis are cars.

# *Scooters*

It's hard not to notice that scooters are the modus operandi for most of the locals. They are plentiful on the road, but it's not as hectic as Thailand— especially if you're out of the city areas and in the quieter parts of Taiwan. To rent a scooter, they require a local motorcycle license. There is an option to rent an electric scooter that accelerates at about half the speed, but you might need to show them a little test that you can be trusted out on the road. If you travel to one of the touristed outlying islands, you'll find the scooter rental rules may relax. They're hard to come across, but there are some companies that allow you to rent a scooter without a motorcycle license. However if you're unsuccessful, there is almost always a company with the electric option close by that you can explore.

## Car Rentals

Renting a car is also an option— one that's not given much attention. Be sure to book in advance and understand that there is a potential that English will be limited with car rental companies. It's likely that car rental companies located at the airport will have better resources for English speakers.

## Private Driver

Another way to see the island is with a private driver. I'm sure you can already see the beauty in this— the ability to curate your own itenary without complicated commutes that soak up time. This option is best for day trips from Taipei like to Yehliu Geopark, Tamsui, Jiufen, etc.

# Climate

*T*aiwan is pretty darn hot. It's kind of like Florida but hotter and equally humid. Honestly the island is so dynamic that you'll experience the climate differently depending on where you are. Generally all of Taiwan reaches high temperatures. It's considered a subtropical climate and August is an unforgivingly hot time. But that is right in the crux of mango season and you do not want to miss mango season in Taiwan! A big part of Taiwan is food; food correlates to seasons, so I personally would grin and bear the outrageous temperatures in order to sink my teeth into some mango *xuě huā bīng*.

Things start to cool down around October for autumn. This is probably the most comfortable season, but how comfortable can you really be without mangos? Ok, I'll leave the mangos behind. For more comfortable temperatures and smaller crowds, November would be a good time to visit.

December through February brings not only winter, but also hot pot season. If you travel during the winter time, it will hardly get cold. Maybe 50 the lowest. But keep in mind that it is colder the higher you travel in altitude. Winters in Taiwan don't get too brutal on the outskirts, but the mountains can definitely be quite cool, respectively. Think low to high 30's Fahrenheit. One thing that really accounts for hotpot's popularity is the traditional medicine philosophies rooted in Taiwan's culture.

If you're invited for dinner with a local, you'll notice they always order balanced meals for the table; a meat, seafood, soup, and vegetable. Balance is necessary to maintain a healthily functioning body. Foods carry energy that is considered either cooling or warming, yin or yang. Traditionally these energies directly correlate to the season an item grows. For example, watermelon is a cooling food, so it will be eaten in summer. Winter seasonal root vegetables would provide the body with warming nourishment. Warming and cooling energies do not always depend on the temperature of a food— it's about how our bodies react with the food internally.

You can also consider late spring from April to May, but keep in mind that it tends to rain more in late spring, which is why the crowds are less. Summer arrives from June to September with a scorching heat. Average temperatures can be as low as 75° F if you're lucky but they tend to hover around the 90's. It's important to note also that summer is typhoon season. There aren't typhoons all the time, but it might lend to more rain in Taiwan if another island nearby is experiencing a typhoon. Personally, I felt it rained more during spring than it did in summer— except for Yilan. It's always raining in Yilan. Beyond that it didn't seem to rain much during the summer months.

## Earthquakes

Oh yea. That reminds me. Speaking of natural phenomenons, Taiwan is also inclined towards earthquakes. Small tremors occur so frequently that locals are often unbothered. Rule of thumb is that if you feel an earthquake lasting more than a minute, then you should exit the building. But really the majority of them are so slight that you have to stop moving and turn off your music in order to feel them.

Through the buzz of my electric tooth brush I hear my roommate ask about an earthquake. Here? Now? She says yes and that she could feel the bed shaking-- in fact she thought maybe I was kicking it. I put my hand down and feel the faint vibrations of a ceasing earthquake. I missed my first earthquake because I was brushing my teeth.

# The Asian Brown Cloud

The smog? It's like stepping out into a foggy morning. Except the fog never lifts. The grey never dissipates because smog isn't water droplets suspended above the ground. Smog clings to the Earth and sticks to your lungs. This is formally known as "The Asian Brown Cloud." In the short term, you don't notice anything, but having lived there for an extended period of time, it littered my lungs and I developed a deep hacking cough I couldn't simply relieve.

All eight of us expats experienced it. It was terrible. During the winter months, pollution blows over from China and gets stuck on the left side of Taiwan's central mountain range, protecting the east coast from unclean air. It's easy to think or just say they're wearing masks for fashion or COVID, but take it from someone who watched the soot rinse out while washing her mask. The pollution is real, and the masks really help. But as I mentioned, it's only concerning over long periods of time, during the winter, and when the air quality index value is high.

# *Staying Connected*

*T*aiwan is remarkably open. The democracy allows access to all social media sites ubiquitous in the U.S. Remember that 7-eleven and Family Mart are your best friends. To call home, you can purchase an international calling card, but calling a landline or cell phone through Skype felt more accessible to me. Alternatively, if you purchased a local sim card for your trip, self-help machines allow for an easy refill.

There is free wifi across the entire island (that you can access with a local Taiwan phone number), but I don't think anyone has the patience to entertain that speed. It will come to a point where you really just rather have a personal hotspot (pocket wifi). You can order one in advance through APTG with unlimited data usage for about NT$100 or a little over USD$3 per day. They even offer delivery to your hotel for a fee of NT$180 (USD$6). If you'd rather not brave google translating all the characters on the site, there's no need to worry. You can pick one up at device rental shops outside of the arrivals area at TPE.

• • •

These are some helpful apps that I recommend having on your phone during your trip:

- **Google Translate.** While Google Translate isn't the best for helping you with proper grammar, it's pretty helpful for getting points or ideas across. My favorite feature to use is the camera for direct translation of restaurant menus. Sometimes you can capture a picture and highlight what you need translated. Other times you can hover over the menu and it will directly translate live without needing to capture an image. Another amazing feature for this app is the speak to translate. You can speak English into it and it will type the characters and speak out the translation instantaneously. You can also flip it so locals can speak to you. This is probably a good time to mention that traditional characters are used in Taiwan, not simplified.

- **Pleco.** Pleco is mostly helpful for those

with a bit of a grasp on the language. It's a dictionary app that makes google translate look like play play. It doesn't have any image-caputre-translate functionality, but its a great dictionary for finding the word you're *actually* looking for.

- **Google Maps** isn't exactly one of the apps I think is dire to have on your phone, but it's not totally worthless. I found it to chart the island better than Apple Maps. Google Maps does not work flawlessly in the same way it does in the United States. Business can be hard to find even if you know the characters to type. Many times you'll come across something that isn't even mapped. Part of that is the pop up culture. Part of it is the mom and pop nature of things. You'll notice places that look more like traditionally established restaurants are more likely to appear on maps. Depending on where you are, the majority of places might not even have searchable English names. If push comes to shove and you're not interested in just wandering around until you see something good or scouring blogs, use the "explore nearby restaurants" feature on Google Maps to scope out some places.

# What to Do

# *Local & Tourist Advice*

*I* hear the familiar jovial jingle of what could only be identified as an ice cream truck, and my heart patters with childhood memories of scraping together coins to chase down the truck and satisfy my sweet tooth. I turn to look and see a large yellow truck. And instead of children with change I see shop owners with trash bags. It was trash collection time. But since we were just talking about ice cream, we might as well dive into food. Street food is the bloodline of Taiwan.

## *Food*

I'm heading straight for the BBQ chicken pizza. I grab a slice and take a bite when Claire asks, "Hey Brittany, what kind of pizza is that?" The moment I open my mouth to answer, my eye zooms in to an opening where the cheese just barely covers something purple. It's not BBQ chicken pizza; that's definitely a tentacle.

On another occasion, my waffle came topped with divine whipped cream, marshmallows, mayo, tomato, and tuna. Did I mention Tai-wan does a lot of strange things? To be fair, I did think I was ordering a waffle with smoked salmon. But I just don't understand why the whipped cream and marshmallow were necessary. It reminds me of that time I accidentally ordered a breakfast hot dog. On a fluffy, flaky baguette came a hotdog, ketchup, mustard, relish, tomato, lettuce and egg. At 8:00 am. I guess egg was the breakfast part. Oh, and the hot chocolate.

Ok, Taiwan does a lot of strange things like put cucumbers and green peas on pizza but we need to have a serious conversation about why French toast grilled cheese is not a thing in the United States. We also need to talk about the meals you must try before leaving...

This brings us back to the mango *xuehua-bing* (芒果雪花冰). If you're blessed to visit during mango season, you need to stop by a dessert shop that serves this decadence. Condensed milk ice is shaved into fluffy snow, topped with mango slic-

*Life changing mango with condensed milk snow ice*
*August 2018*

es and if the stars are aligned, drizzled with more condensed milk. I don't know what exactly we have been doing in the United States with these crunchy snow cones, but you *need* to experience the pillowy goodness of **Taiwanese snow ice.**

There are a few things people in Taiwan will fight about. One of them is which is the best **pineapple cake** and the other is where to sip the best **beef noodle soup.** They are some of Taiwan's prides. The best pineapple cakes I had were from Jun-Mei. I would argue that these are the best in Taiwan. And I've had a lot of pineapple cake in Taiwan. As for beef noodle soup （牛肉麵）, I wish I knew how lucky I was after the first bite at the restaurant we randomly chose for dinner. I would not again encounter beef so tender and broth so robust for my remaining 10 months in Taiwan.

The simplicity of *Luó ròu fàn* （螺肉飯） comforts the heart as a traditional meal serving braised pork over steamed rice garnished with modest green vegetables and half of a boiled egg. A bowl typically sells for about NT$60, hovering around USD$2. It's one of my favorites.

**Hotpot** （火鍋） is another fan favorite. My favorite thing about hot pot is how absolutely luxurious your meal can look for less than USD$10. But in essence hot pot is DIY soup. It is good, but I'm not a hot pot fanatic. I've heard the Orange Shabu Shabu House in Taipei has quite the reign on this delicacy.

Not everyone is a fan of soy milk, but I found the warm feeling of homemade *dòu jiāng* （豆漿） in the mornings quickly growing on me. I particularly became a fan of black tea with soy milk—the downfall is that it's not a consistent flavor that you can confidently order everywhere.

Did I mention they love putting fruits in milk? Don't be alarmed when you see apple milk and banana milk in 7-eleven. You won't find those much in night markets, but you will definitely run into papaya milk. It's pretty good. Not too creamy and not too sweet—you usually have the option to adjust your sweetness level as well.

You'll notice tea shops are ever present. Ordering tea was nothing like the lessons in school. Be prepared for a mountain of questions. After you communicate the flavor of tea you like, they will ask the ice level, sweetness level, and confirm the beverage size or number of beverages. If you're looking for a nearly fool proof ordering method, type in the details on Google Translate: "medium cup, half sugar, regular ice" and use the speech translation option. If internet isn't accessible for you, when you're at your accommodation you can use internet there to record

Boba & vanilla cream wheel cake

December 2018

the Google translation speech and screenshot the text to save in an easily accessible album photo in your photos. The third option is copying and pasting the characters into a note on your phone, or writing them down in the journal section of this book so you can show them every time.

*Guà bāo* (刈包), also referred to as the **"Taiwanese hamburger,"** is a braised pork belly sandwich garnished with pickled vegetables, coriander, and peanut powder between two halves of a steamed bun. You can scope out one these delicious snacks in night markets, but again not everyone has mastered the *guà bāo* art.

**Wheel Cakes** are something you really should let your tastebuds meet. It's essentially a stuffed pancake, but they come with assorted fillings from sweet red bean to chocolate, vanilla custard or cheese. That's not an exhaustive list.

**Scallion pancakes** （蔥油餅） are also a good breakfast choice. Well really, you can snag one for any meal. My favorite variation of this is the *zhuā bing* （抓餅）. It's a scallion pancake prepared by a method that creates a flaky quality. This pan fried dough is layered with chopped green onion. If you're lucky, you'll buck up into a stall that is serving these stuffed. At the Fenjia night market in Taichung, a vendor sells this irresistible teriyaki pork *lào bing* （照燒豬排蛋烙餅）. A *lào bing* is pretty similar to *zhuā bing* and *cōng yóubing*, but the changes are mainly in the absence of scallion and preparation methods that determine texture.

If you spend enough time in Taiwan you'll come to know that lunch boxes are loved by the locals, as they are stuffed with the epitome of Taiwanese comfort foods. Typically these boxes come with steamed rice, pork and chicken or maybe fish, and a variety of vegetable options.

This island has truly found a way to exploit the versatility of soybeans. Even so, vegetarian meals are difficult to come by because near-one 一

two 丁

three 下

four 下

five 正

ly everything will have a bit of meat in it. There is a chance for vegetarians but vegan food is rare. A delicious option is **sesame noodles**.

I pride myself on always having A+ food recommendations and *dòuhuā* （豆花） isn't something on my personal list, but is a popular dessert in Taiwan that you should feel free to try. Again, I am not endorsing it, but recommend you have the experience. It's a sweet tofu pudding that is served in a number of ways with toppings that range from beans to tapioca pearls or peanuts.

Stinky tofu really is a thing. Named *chòu dòufu* （臭豆腐), you will smell it before you see it. Always. It will overwhelm your nose while walking through the night markets and you will catch yourself wondering what on this green earth is that *smell*? But don't knock it till you try it! I tried it first, and then knocked it. Ok, it wasn't entirely that bad. It tasted kind of like cheese. It was most tolerable for me when eaten with a heaping serving of the pickled vegetables that nearly disguised the whole stinky tofu flavor.

Because the culture is rooted in family style meals, when you order from a restaurant, you'll likely notice boxes on the side of the menu. This is to denote how many orders of an item you would like. There's a special way these are filled. It's kind of like the tally system we have where the fifth line is struck diagonally. Same concept, but looks way cooler.

Remember, you always have the option of pointing at the menu item and then holding up your fingers to say how many.

If you're looking for a quick breakfast one morning or a light snack to hold you over in between meals, don't bat your eyelash at the convenience stores, they have some delectables there. If you're really easy-going you can munch on a tea egg for only NT$10, grab a roasted sweet potato, or maybe even that chicken and caramelized onion egg and rice wrap that you can find in the fridge section and have heated. Not everything can be heated, so they might look at you strangely if you bring them the noodles with cucumbers, carrots, and sesame sauce. But items that are heated have an indicator icon on the packaging.

If you pick up something to eat at a Family Mart, 7-eleven, or other small convenience store and the teller says something to you when you hand it over to pay, they're likely asking if you want them to heat the item. They will ask you, *jiārè ma* （加熱嗎）? To be honest, I don't actually know what the "correct" response to that is. Typically the language format is confirming the verb. So in English that sounds like "Heat it up?" "Heat it up," instead of yes or no. That's why I would believe it's *jiārè* （加熱） but you can also say *hǎo* （好） which means ok, or good. You can't go wrong with nodding your head either.

Note that the Taiwanese are serious about recycling. Food is separated from boxes, boxes are washed and stacked, and separated from chopsticks, and the plastic cup for your tea.

You might have heard not to leave your chopsticks standing in your food. Upright chopsticks resemble incenses and the spirits may believe you are intending an offering. You are not meant to consume your offerings, and standing chopsticks in your food is a serious offense. When not in use, simply lay them flat across the bowl or to the side.

# Spiritual Celebrations

The Taiwanese are serious about their relationship to the gods. Living directly across from a temple was cool until you realize just how extravagant their spirituality is. One time, a small earthquake caused some things to fall in one of the temples on my street and they blocked off the entire stretch to throw a celebration asking to return to the diety's grace. A goat and pig spread on a stake with fruit through their mouths. A shaman dances. An endless array of ornate baskets with fruits, foods, and beer line eighty tables. Puppeteers perform for the gods. It's colorful. And absolutely and completely extra in every way. The Taiwanese do not play. They really go all out. I never experienced a confetti cannon in my life. But in just 11 months of living in Taiwan, I'd been in three.

From the office I hear music and look up to see what looked like another funeral procession. Another framed photo dawned with flowers, another brigade of cars. Then I see the familiar banner of a political candidate and realize it was a publicity campaign. They stand in the flatbed of a moving truck, smiling and waving. Then several gunshots. Smoke everywhere. Wait. They were firecrackers, not gunshots. I forgot I was no longer in a country plagued with rampant gun violence.

Plumes of smoke rise into the air as locals burn money for the gods and their ancestors. Around August and September during the 7th lunar month, Ghost Month begins. It's a tradition for both Taoists and Buddhists. To escape misfortune, some activities must be avoided. During Ghost Month, neglected spirits might become mischievous, and play pranks on the living. One of the vengeful tricks is switching places— the mortal returns to the underworld, while the spirit stays in the here and now. A handful of activities are therefore inauspicious during Ghost Month, most of which do not affect casual travelers like moving, starting a new business, or getting married. However, there is one thing. It is said that you should not swim in large bodies of water because a spirit may drag you away. If you're not one to mind their Ghost Month taboos, you'll find beaches, lakes, and pools easy to navigate as followers of the tradition believe the spirits of the drowned will try to trap swimmers souls in the water. The beaches will be far less crowded.

For visitors looking to experience Ghost Month festivities, Keelung has large and colorful celebrations. Ghost lanterns illuminate to help guide the path for visiting spirits. Operas, puppet shows, and live singing fill the temples. Keelung is the home of a temple extremely important to Ghost Month as a set of its doors is believed to be a doorway to the underworld. There they hold the Kanmen Ritual（開龕門）; it opens the gate to commemorate the beginnings of Ghost Month.

On the 14th day of the 7th month, a festival of water lanterns draws celebration and parades fill streets. Late in the moonlight, house-shaped paper lanterns are stuffed with ghost money and led to Badouzi Harbor, set aflame and watched as they drift atop the water. The longer they last and remain afloat, the more auspicious the new year will be.

# *Things to Do*

"*T*aiwanese *people* love standing in lines."

It didn't occur to me until my friend pointed out how often you'll see a cue for something, not necessarily because it's good, but because it's famous. Personally I'm the no nonsense type. I don't care much if it's famous, I care more about the culinary flair.

What is there to *do* in Taiwan? Locals love traveling the island. It's mostly to eat a geospecific delicacy, take photos with famous landmarks, or hike. The hiking is really casual. You will see people dressed in nearly formal outfits walking through tangled roots and moss covered rocks, sometimes only wearing flip flops. They adore natural photo shoots so if you're also interested in that lifestyle, you will fit right in. Not everyone hiking is doing this, but its really not an uncommon occurence.

There's such a supportive spirit during these activities. Hiking up as someone hikes down, there's a good chance they'll greet you by saying *jiāyóu* (加油). The direct translation is "add oil" but it's just a boost of encouragement that has no direct English translation. I like to think of it as saying "Hustle, you got this!"

"Closed since 2016 due to landslides," the print insists as we follow the locals past warning signs we can't read, through the cave, up the trail and down to the waterfall. A kind woman shares there are two more waterfalls and tells the trail. Through overgrown roots and outrageous rock placement, we arrive at the second clearing that more closely resembles rapids where a makeshift bridge strung together with one plank of wood and a few rocks tempts the other side. We see hikers across the way and confirm the sign that we are meant to cross. We take off our shoes and dip toes into the cold water, stand on the slippery rocks, fall off the slippery rocks. Oh no! I feel Rachel grabbing on to my back so the current doesn't drag me away.

If any form of hiking sounds undesirable to you, another lovely pastime is bicycling. Some abandoned places have been repurposed as bike trails and there's always the option to ride around the city. YouBike rental sites are stationed in a plethora of cities around the island. It's a bit tedious to use because you cannot register for a YouBike account without an identification number— the options are Identity Card, Alien Resident Card, or none of the above. Without an account, you can't pay by EasyCard. You can however still use one without registering for an account and linking it to your EasyCard card by selecting a bike as a one-time-rental. This requires you to directly enter your credit card information at the kiosk each time. Every thirty minutes for the first four hours is charged at NT$10. If your ride extends into the next four hours, the charge increases to NT$20 per 30 minutes. Rides exceeding eight hours double to NT$40 per 30 minutes.

• • •

You don't have to worry about scams or dishonesty, but know that you can haggle. If shopping at a farmers market with a street vendor, you can ask for "bundle pricing" - a lower price because you're purchasing a number of items. As a general rule, if you're able to bargain for it, a receipt likely won't accompany your purchase. To encourage honest book keeping, there's a receipt lottery. On the top of your receipts you'll notice a QR code that you can scan to check for winning codes.

Take your money and get a massage in

Taiwan. Now listen, and listen carefully. I do not, under any circumstances, recommend you to receive a foot massage. Get the shoulder and/or back massage instead. The foot massages are a front for a human tenderizing business. It seems like inflicting pain to rid of pain is counter productive, but they are well versed in foot reflexology and traditional medicine revolving energy meridians, so all of the torture might not be in vain. But, I would not wish a Taiwanese foot massage on my worst enemy.

• • •

What about Taiwan's night life? To be quite honest, I'm not the best to advise on nightlife because I have a pretty strict 8 pm bed time. But here is the little bit I do know.

KTV is the nightlife. People in Taiwan absolutely love it. A group of friends will rent out a private karaoke room and holler at the top of their lungs through laughter and bites of food. This is by far the most popular night life activity in Taiwan. This is not karaoke night at some dive but at well-dressed venues specifically dedicated to this endeavor. You will be pleased to know that there are a number of English song selections with accompanying music videos that are lacking in no cringe factor. I would also be remiss not to mention their selection of English songs are exclusively from the late 20th century and early 2000's. The nostalgia is great for throwback night.

Wait, did I say KTV was the night life? I meant to say the night markets are the night life. And I don't even mean that facetiously. People flock to night markets for quick bites. There's a big "eating out" culture in Taiwan that pulls crowds at night. In fact, it's practically cheaper to eat out than to cook your own meals. Plus with the convenience? Say Less. Depending on the size of the night market, you'll find a lot more than food there. Vendors will open their stores of clothes, accessories, or beauty products and some have carnival style games to play. The night market can be a dynamic experience.

Sometimes you might hear expats living here grouch that there is no nightlife. It's not that there is none, it's that their night life looks very different from our own. When Americans consider whether or not somewhere has nightlife, they envision clubs and bars. Beyond KTV and night markets, you will find that the club and bar nightlife mostly in Taipei. Because clubs are not a huge part of the culture, they are relatively pricey. Cover fees hover around US$30 I would recommend saving it for more orders of bubble tea, but I loved seeing how alive and well the dance culture is in Taiwan. Right now, early 2000's styles are trending. Think baggy t-shirts and jeans. Circular cyphers with breakdancing and popping. You might not find it everywhere, but I found it more than I would have ever imagined.

The bars would probably be the next best thing. But keep in mind the atmosphere won't be one so much centered on meeting and connecting with strangers. Usually when people in Taiwan have a night on the town, it's with a larger group of friends rather than small squads of three or the sort. It's a more muted energy, relaxed and based on strengthening existing relationships.

# Major Attractions

## Sun Moon Lake 日月潭

Sun Moon Lake is something from an island paradise fairy tale. Taiwan's largest body of water is nestled in the foothills of the island's central mountain range, surrounded by lush vegetation. This almost mystical body of water is home to the Thao aboriginal people. There you'll find a trail rated by CNN Travel as one of the "Top Ten Bike Trails to Take Your Breath Away in The World." If you arrive in early spring, you just might catch the cherry blossoms.

# *Alishan* 阿里山

Then there's the mystic atmosphere of Alishan, an old world dense with towering trees and sacred spaces. This national park is Taiwan's most visited, as travelers flock to experience the magnificent spread of centuries old Giant Red Cypress Trees, hiking trails, and a scarlet narrow-gauge train from a bygone era. At these altitudes, Alishan has also garnered a reputation for its tea. Travelers wake up to greet the sun as it ascends over the crest of nearby mountain peaks. I'll be real with you, that sunrise is the most elusive and infamous of them all. I spoke with locals that said they tried four separate times and have never succeeded in seeing the Alishan Sunrise. I asked a number of different people around my homestay whether it was worth it to chase Alishan's sunrise and no one responded enthusiastically about it. "Why don't you watch the sunrise from this other local spot?" We drive the winding road that takes us up into the midrange of the mountains and to a family's tea farm where a sign reads "sunrise lookout." We walk gingerly through the morning dew, careful not to slip on moss-covered rocks. Perching at the top of the hill, we wait for the sun to make its way up into the sky. Just as it nearly peaks over the edge of the mountains, clouds swoop in, blocking the moment we woke so early for. I never felt traveler's remorse. Our moment was beautiful.

The journey to Alishan isn't an easy one for a couple of reasons. One is the process of traveling inland and the other is because there are so many ways to get there, with so little English information. While you can go directly to Alishan in one day from Taipei, it would require aggressive traveling. It seems like a better idea to travel down to Chaiyi the day before, settle in with some turkey rice, and then get ready to set out before the break of dawn for the famous sunrise. If your budget is more expansive, you could have the luxury of staying at an accommodation inside the park— it saves you from waking up excruciatingly early and includes a shuttle ride to the summit.

The sunrise actually happens on an adjacent mountain called Chusan, which is why you have to take a separate train from Alishan to Chusan station. There you'll reach an elevation of 7,897ft which allows you to catch an amazing outlook at the surrounding mountains range. The position of the sunrise changes according to the seasons, so keep that in mind when picking your vantage point. In the winter the sun rises towards the right and in the summer it will appear slightly left.

The easiest method to acquire tickets involves staying at a hotel that sells sunrise tickets so you don't have to visit the park's ticket booth the day before. They only sell sunrise tickets the day before between the hours of 1 PM and 4:30 PM, so it's not the easiest errand to slip into your day. Here, they will also announce the sunrise time so you can plan your morning transportation. I would strongly recommend staying at the Alishan House just for the sheer convenience— complimentary shuttle service to and from the train station, convenient sunrise train ticket purchasing, brilliant guest suites, decadent breakfast buffets, and a sample of the region's famous tea. Alternatively, there's an observation deck with a scenic outlook, not too shabby for watching the sunrise— just know that this technically would not count as *the* Alishan sunrise.

There are 5 major pieces to an Alishan trip: Number 1 is the sunrise. Number 2 is the Alishan. And the Forest Railway, sunset, sea clouds, and forest trails complete the experiene. The hiking trails range from moderate to relaxed and can be completed in as little as an hour. A red train travels throughout the park taking visitors from one trail to another. Before you decide to add this excursion in your itinerary it's important to use these different facets of the Alishan experience to guide your planning process. Which of these 5 things means the most to you? You should probably plan on using 2 days to put Alishan into your itinerary.

On your way to Alishan, there's a pitstop town called Fenqihu. This old town was formerly a refueling area for trains heading up to Alishan. If this town is part of your trip, be sure to take a bite out of a Fenqihu bento box. A white beard-ed man holding a jolly thumbs up with his right hand and an embossed metal lunch tin in the left will be plastered on signage leading to the restaurant. True to the lunch box style you'll find all around Taiwan, these are filled with a pork chop and chicken leg lain on a bed of rice accompanied by a tea egg and both preserved and fresh vegetables. This is also an opportunity to pick up a souvenir! If you'd like you can make your NT$120 meal NT$300 and keep the authentic metal bento container.

# Green Island 綠島

Green Island is a magical place. We spent our time scooting around the auxiliary island sandwiched between the mountains and sea with vivid greens and blues, hues you'd think were photoshopped. It's become a tourist hotspot for its deep blues and greens, not to mention amazing scuba diving. This is your launch site to reach the world's deepest underwater mailbox. And get this, you can send real mail there with specially made waterproof postcards designed by local schoolchildren.

# Water and Fire Cave 水火同源

There really is a cave where fire dances on top of the water. It stems from a natural hot spring as a result of a fissure that releases both water and natural gas, from the Liuchong River Fault running underneath the ground. Tainan's Guanziling resort village also has quite the reputation for its hot springs. Travelers admire the seemingly ideal location—tucked in verdant mountains yet close to a city and major transportation hubs.

# *Taipei* 臺北

If you decide to stay in Taipei, take the Elephant Mountain hiking trail for beautiful city views. It's a short hike, but 20 minutes of walking up steep stairs. Along the trail there are plenty of rest benches. Elephant Mountain is in the collection of trails that make up the Four Beasts Mountains. Many just ascend to the Six Giant Rocks, snap some iconic photos of the skyline, and then head back down. I recommend an early morning or sunset trek— but keep in mind that sunset will likely be busy.

The most prominent building you'll see from the lookout at Elephant Mountain is Taipei 101. Taipei 101, once the world's tallest building, stretches into the sky with architecture inspired by the shape of bamboo. Located just 660ft from a major fault line, it's the tallest building with such proximity to an earthquake zone. Consequently, the architecture needed to be deliberate in earthquake resistance. Several ropes hang a steel pendulum between floors 88 and 87, known as a tuned mass damper. When the

Fengjia night market, Taichung
September 2018

building experiences strong winds or disruption from earthquakes, the pendulum swings in the direction opposite to the sway of the building, reducing the overall displacement. This is what allows the 1,667ft tall building, approximately the length of two football fields, to withstand an earthquake rated 9 on the Richter scale. In its fortress, you'll find shopping and dining, in addition to an observation deck.

On the 91st floor is an open-air terrace that allows 360 degree views of the city. This is one of the highest open-air observation decks in the world and one of the few skyscrapers that have hosted concerts on its rooftop. Level 101 houses the Summit 101 VIP club, a lounge similar to the 103rd floor of the Empire State Building exclusive for celebrities, however ordinary people have the ability to access Summit 101. They'll just need to show receipts of their purchases exceeding one million New Taiwan dollars from their shopping spree in the Taipei 101 Mall—that's about USD$34,000. If you're looking for a way to pass the time that's much easier on your wallet, gardens and temples honor Taiwan's first president at Chiang Kai-shek Memorial Hall where you can watch the changing of the guards.

# Fo Guang Shan 佛光山

In Kaohsiung, the buddhist monastery Fo Guang Shan carves into the side of a mountain with unimaginable grandeur. Through the clouds shine golden rays that highlight the serenity and peace settled in this red and gold commune. The energy invites reflection. It is the resting place of Taiwan's largest Buddha, who sits 356 feet tall including his chair at the crest of a short hill.

Along the path down to the concourse underneath the Sakyamuni Buddha are eight pagodas, symbolizing the Noble Eightfold Path. However, the most iconic pagodas of Kaohsiung are the Dragon and Tiger pagodas jutting into Lotus Lake.

## Taroko Gorge 太魯閣

Taroko Gorge is a stunning canyon stretching 12 miles throughout Taroko National Park. The rugged coastal cliffs formed by the Liwu River have created the world's deepest marble canyon— and an oasis for travelers from its subtropical forested canyons to the peaks lucious with subalpine coniferous forests.

## Kenting National Park 墾丁國家公園

The pristine beaches of Kenting National Park occupy the southern tip of Taiwan. Surrounded by lush forest and white sand beaches contrasted against deep blue waters, sunset is a symphony of colors. You could spend three days traversing the attractions. Rent a scooter and visit Hengchun town, stopping to admire the four old city gates and eat your way through the night market. Watch the clouds float by in Maobito Park. Explore the caves, coral reefs and northern mountains. Access Kenting National Park via bus in Kaohsiung either by the Zuoying HSR station or Kaohsiung Main Station. To give you an indication of how coveted the views at Kenting National Park are, the buses depart about every 30 minutes— and it's a two and a half hour drive.

# *Sample Itinerary*

*H*onestly, you need a minimum of **two weeks** to travel Taiwan respectably. That's why I've included the "The Ultimate Taiwan Trip" option at the end. However if you want a quick 5 day trip, here are a few itineraries to consider.

If you're very anxious about language, I recommend you adhere to the "Taipei Main" plan. It gives you a glimpse of the natural beauty within proximity to the city. There is a high expat population in the capital city so finding restaurants with English speaking servers and menus is rather easy.

"Off Taipei" is for those travelers who are hoping to experience much smaller crowds and travel the Taipei area in an "off the beaten path" type of way. There will be a marginally smaller English crutch, but I would consider these destinations still very accessible to those with no language expertise.

Technically speaking, Airbnb is illegal in Taiwan. That does not mean you can't find bookings on the website. However, I've noticed that

Airbnb hosts tend to price higher than the average for accommodations. I almost exclusively used booking.com to find hotels, hostels, homestays, and B&Bs. I feel obligated to mention Agoda, but in my experience, their prices are disrespectful.

# Taipei Main

"Taipei Main" is a visit to **Jiufen**, a prosperous gold mining town during Japanese occupation turned enchanting tourist attraction, famous for inspiring the imagery in Miyazaki's "Spirited Away." Launch a sky lantern with wishes or explore the Japanese gold mine remnants. Find adventure in the labyrinth of alleyways. It's one of the most popular destinations in Taiwan as its hillside with lantern lined streets attracts quite the crowd. These red lanterns and calligraphy signs contour deep jade and persimmon buildings jutting out from the incline. Travel to Jiufen for the local foods and tea at a famous tea house. Be warned that the streets here will be crowded. Very crowded. A bus leaves Jiufen taking riders back to Zhongxiao Fuxing Station, with the last leaving around 6:00pm. Something to keep in mind is that the line for this last call starts early and can get pretty long. If you miss the bus, you can always hail a taxi back to the city.

To build your giant sky lantern from scratch, you'll want to stop in **Shifen**. Shifen is dense with people hoping to enjoy the quaint village where shops, cafes, and restaurants border railroad tracks. It is a popular spot for flying paper lanterns that send wishes and goals into the skies. There you'll find Taiwan's widest waterfall: the Niagara of Taiwan.

For swinging rope bridges and three waterfalls, take the friendly **Sandiaoling Waterfall Hike** on a day trip out of Taipei. It's a remote trail without amenities, so be sure to pack plenty of refreshments. The trailhead is easy to access from the Sandiaoling Train Station. Direct trains leave approximately once an hour. If that's not a convenient time, you can take a multi-step route, riding to Ruifang and making a transfer to the Pingxi Line to disembark at Sandiaoling. The direct train ticket will cost about NT$60, just around USD$2. You can walk to Shifren from the waterfall hike, or you can take the Doha train station one stop.

An hour ride from Taipei Main Station gives you a glimpse into the quieter nature of Taiwan as you head to the **National Palace Museum** and see the mountain side of Taipei's city life.

Remember when Chiang Kai-shek fled to Taiwan after the Chinese Civil War? Well, he packed about 20 percent of the palace's imperial treasures in his suitcase, creating an exhibition with the largest number of ancient Chinese artifacts, exceeding Beijing's Forbidden City.

**Maji Square** is a sort of adult playground located in the Taipei Expo Park's Yushan Park Area and a five minute walk from the Yushan MRT station. It's farmers market meet artisan anti-mall with an open design concept where breeze wafts the aroma of meals and sound of chatter. At night, the bar scene comes to life. The market is sourced from a slew of recycled material: wooden pallets, card containers, discarded military tents. This gives you and idea of the rebellious artisanship of the architecture. It is chic and stylish. It is eco-friendly. It is a testament to the notion that those concerns remain at the core of youth's society in Taiwan.

**Four Four South Village** is Maji Square's cousin. The former military residential area has become a cultural and creative market, preserving its history through an on-site museum. It boasts proximity to Taipei 101.

You need to peruse a night market. **Shilin Night Market** is probably the most famous night market in Taiwan, and because of that, you'll notice it will draw quite the crowd. **Tonghua Night Market (Linjiang Street Night Market)** , located accessibly in the downtown area, is a good alternative. If you're really not interested in squeezing your way though the crowds at Shilin and all the food choices overwhelming, **Jing Mei Market** is a more modest option.

**Din Tai Fung** is like a staple culinary affair. It's a Michelin star restaurant famous for their dim sum. *Xiǎolóng bāo* should be on your order. They even serve chocolate dumplings there! If for some reason you're like me and have an adventurous spirit with thick skin to withstand uncomfortable situations, head to **Modern Toilet**. It's a toilet themed restaurant. Beverages are served in urinals and curry in toilet bowls while you sit on a toilet seat. Oh wait, I didn't mention Taiwan kind of has a thing for themed restaurants did I? There's also **Houtong Cat Village** and a Hello Kitty themed restaurant. While we are here, I would be remiss not to mention, **Miyahara Ice Cream Parlor.**

# Off Taipei

If you can't make it over to Taroko National Park, the 45 minute bus ride to **Wulai** just might scratch your gorge itch. You can catch the NT$15 Bus 849 near Xindian MRT station. To be honest, it's really bad manners for me to even insinuate that Wulai can in any way compare to Taroko. Taroko is phenomenal. But this quaint village should not be underestimated. A trip to Wulai is a glimpse into the "real" Taiwan. Its an aboriginal village outside of Taipei for the Atayal people. There are hot springs, scenic hiking tails, gorgeous views, and delicious food. It's a change of pace from the bustle of internationally famous attractions in Taipei. In Wulai you can take a gondola up the mountain to steal panoramic views of the beautiful waterfall.

Wulai's hot springs can be found in outdoor pools along the Nanshih river or at a hot spring hotel. I was actually disheartened to realize that most of the hot springs in Taiwan were not in the wild, but at a hot spring hotel. There are some that make the experience lovely, but others that just feel too commercial. The wild hot springs are not on Google Maps. You have to know someone who knows the way. Hot spring hotels usually show prices at the entrance, but you can budget between NT$300- NT$500 (USD$10-$15) for unlimited time at a public pool or book a private room or tub for NT$600-NT$1200 (USD$20-40).

This is probably a good time to talk about hot spring etiquette. Hot springs are not a place for swimming. They're a place for sitting. Think of it as a hot tub. You don't swim in a hot tub— but that's probably because of the size. It's a very relaxed activity. Be sure you never let the water cover your chest, especially not your heart. After 20-30 minutes, take a break and step out of the water to rest on the ledge.

Hot springs come in different flavors, each enhanced by varying minerals with therapeutic properties. In addition to mineral composition, the pools come in different temperatures so you can tempt fate by soaking in extremely cold, dipping in extrmely hot, and feeling imaginary needles pricking your skin. Those with heart disease, high blood pressure, or any open wounds are probably better off skipping the hot springs.

Another thing. Most of the hot springs I went to were bathing suit based with an option for the um, "more natural," hot springs. As a Black woman, I would strongly recommend skipping the naked hot spring in Taiwan and save it for Japan. I never went to a nude hot spring in Taiwan, but I did see the way people responded to my presence in a swimsuit, so I'd imagine nudity would drive either everyone out of the place or draw way more eyes than I'd like. But Japan.

Believe it or not, that is the most comfortable place for anyone to soak in the nude because everyone is really just minding their own business. You almost forget you're technically an "other" but this book isn't about Japan.

The reflection of green mountains and warm lights in the lake of **Bitan Scenic Area** make for a romantic scene. The east and west bank are joined by the pedestrian suspension bridge that resembles a rainbow above the renowned jade waters. The west bank hosts ancient temples, hiking trails, and cliffs while the east is home to a riverside marketplace of container restaurants and promenade to view art installations. An old street night market, sprawling with an array of Taiwanese and pan-Chinese specialties established in the Qing Dynasty, lives on. Ride the historic human-powered ferry, rent a swan boat or paddle board, and take a ride through the gentle slopes of an undulating bikeway. Tour the **Liugongzun Monument Water Park**. Walk **Lion Head Mountain** hiking trail. Entrances are available from Zhongxin Road, Wenzhong Road and Changchun Road where you can reach **Mt. Shitou** and overlook the entire **Xindian area**. Board the green line MRT from Taipei Main Station 40 minutes to the terminus, Xindian, and you will be in the heart of Bitan Scenic Area. The bus to

Wulai also stops directly next to Bitan Scenic Area at the Xindian Station.

Between MRT Longshan Temple Station and Ximen Station on the blue line is a place brimming with history preserved in the 18th century—**Wanhua District**. It's the cradle of Taipei's history. There are six key attractions to consider in this area, accessible by walking tour: **Longshan Temple**, the adjacent night market, **Herbal Lane** outside the temple's east wall with open-faced shops of different teas and over 100 herbs packed tightly into a narrow lane, the clustered heritage architecture from the Qing Dynasty through Japanese colonial era on **Bopiliao Historic Block, Xinfu Market**, and the two remaining structures from the Largest Japanese style Buddhist temple built during the Japanese period at **Xibenyuan Temple Square**.

The red brick buildings of a former wine factory transformed into an artisan venue for cultural events and exhibitions, installations, theater productions and performances. That is **Huashan 1914 Creative Park**. The structures house specialty food stores, cafes, and hand-made gift shops. What makes this creative market different from the others? The maverick knickknacks.

I consider myself a skeleton traveler. Meaning I like to create the frame of my trip but not fill in the minutia. This allows space for spontaneity, for connecting with other travelers or building meaningful interactions with locals. I fear jam packing a schedule creates stressors while life is trying to flow and unfold beautifully with you. For you. That's why I recommend keeping to a more relaxed schedule. Keep a few must-sees or must-dos on a priority list and then fill in the spaces time permitting. Listen to your body. Let it relax when it needs, because what we don't need is you returning from vacation more exhausted from stressful travels. Traveling doesn't need to be action-packed. It's healthy to release the fear that you're not doing enough or that you're not taking advantage of all the time you have. Allow yourself to move with the flow of synchronicity and trust that you will experience all that you're meant to. Allow yourself to fully experience the moment. Every moment. Accept changes to plans gracefully as guidance towards something better or protection from something worse. Understand that each and every memory you make aligns with your best interest.

# Taipei Main

# Day 1

## National Palace Museum
Time to spend there: 2 hours
Entrance fee: NT$50 (USD$12)
Expenses: transportation (bus NT$30, uber ~NT$350);
  optional audio tour (NT$120)
Distance: 6 mi / 10 km from Taipei Main Station

## Shilin Night Market
Time to spend there: 1 hour
Entrance fee: free
Expenses: transportation (bus NT$15, uber ~ NT$300);
  personal meals/shopping
Distance: 2.6 mi/ 4.2 km from National Palace Museum or 5 mi/ 8.1 km from Taipei Main Station

# Day 2

**Jiufen**
Time to spend there: half a day
Entrance fee: free
Expenses: transportation (train & bus NT$64,
uber ~ NT$1,100) personal meals/ shopping
Distance: 26 mi/ 41.1km from Taipei Main
Station

Or
**Shifen**
Time to spend there: half a day
Entrance fee: free
Expenses: transportation (train NT$71, uber ~
NT$1,000)
Distance: 24mi/ 39 km from Taipei Main Station

# Day 3
## Recharge

# Day 4

**Taroko Gorge**

Time to spend there: half a day
Entrance fee: free*
Expenses: transportation
Distance: 111mi/ 178 km from Taipei Main Station

*with the exception of a NT$ 200 fee to enter Zhuilu Old Road*

# *D*ay 5

**Maji Square**
Time to spend there: 2 hours
Entrance fee: free
Expenses: transportation (train ~ NT$ 20); personal shopping & meals
Distance: 2 mi/ 2.9 km from Taipei Main Station

Or
**Four Four South Village & Taipei 101**
Time to spend there: 2 hours
Entrance fee: free*
Expenses: transportation (train ~ NT$ 20); personal shopping & meals
Distance: 4 mi/ 6.5 km from Taipei Main Station

*Entrance fee for Taipei 101 observatory is NT$ 600*

# Off Taipei

# Day 1

**Baitan Scenic Area**
Time to spend there: half a day
Entrance fee: free
Expenses: transportation; accommodations;
meals

# Day 2

**Wulai Gorge**
Time to spend there: half a day
Entrance fee: free
Expenses: transportation; meals; hot spring
entrance

# Day 3
## Recharge

# *D*ay 4

**Wanhua District**
Time to spend there: half a day
Entrance fee: free
Expenses: transportation; personal shopping/
meals

# *D*ay 5

**Huashan 1914 Creative Park**
Time to spend there: half a day
Entrance fee: free
Expenses: transportation; personal shopping/
meals

# *The Ultimate Taiwan Trip*

# *D*ay 1

**Shilin Night Market**
Time to spend there: 2 hours
Entrance fee: free
Expenses: transportation; personal meals/ shopping

# *D*ay 2

**Sun Moon Lake**
Time to spend there: whole day
Entrance fee: NT$300
Expenses: transportation; ferry voucher (NT$300) ; meals; accommodations; Formosan Aboriginal Culture Village access pass

# *D*ay 3
**Taichung City Recharge**

# Day 4

**Alishan National Scenic Area**
Time to spend there: whole day
Entrance fee: NT$300
Expenses: transportation (in park train); accommodations; meals

# Day 5
**Recharge**

# Day 6

**Fo Guang Shan Buddhist Museum and Monastery**
Time to spend there: 2 hours
Entrance fee: free
Expenses: transportation; meals (they offer an extensive vegetarian buffet)

**Kaohsiung Lotus Pond**
Time to spend there: 2 hours
Entrance Fee: free
Expenses: transportation; souvenir shopping

# Day 7

**Kenting National Park**
Time to spend there: whole day
Entrance Fee: free*
Expenses: transportation; accommodation;
meals
*6 out of the 10 sections require an entrance fee ranging from*
*NT$ 30 per person to NT$ 150 per person*

# Day 8
## Taitung City recharge

# Day 9

**Green Island**
Time to spend there: whole day
Entrance Fee: free
Expenses: transportation (ferry NT$ 980 round
trip); accommodation; meals; activities (snorkel-
ing/ scuba diving/ scooter rental)

# Day 10
## Return from Green Island/ Travel

# Day 11
## Hualien Recharge

# Day 12

**Taroko National Park**
Time to spend there: whole day
Entrance Fee: free*
Expenses: transportation (train or bus); accommodation; meals
*with the exception of a NT$ 200 fee to enter Zhuilu Old Road*

# Day 13

**Jiufen**
Time to spend there: half a day
Entrance fee: free
Expenses: transportation (train & bus) personal meals/ shopping

# $\mathcal{D}$ay 14
## Taipei Recharge

• • •

You'll notice that I've left a few days as recharge days. That is whatever recharge means for you. Maybe it's a day meandering through a park you've spotted, riding a bike through the area, or people watching at a cafe. Usually when we travel we plan the schedule to every waking second and don't allow a time or space for replenishing all the energy that traversing unfamiliar territory drains. Make of these days what you want— whether that's sprinkling them with excursions to other places I've mentioned throughout your read, or relaxing for a few hours at your accommodation.

The idea of a recharge day is that you spend time recuperating, also known as doing nothing at all. There's this belief that when we travel we must "get the most" out of our trip. Not only is that untrue, but it's also unhealthy. It allows guilt to creep in when your body is tired and really just needs to relax. Being honest with your body and allowing yourself to feel your truth is so important. As a high functioning introvert, people find themselves shocked to realize how much recharge time I need. Accept your truth and live in it boldly, because what we don't need is to invite the feeling of guilt where our self-care should be.

On these days you can do nothing at all and relax in bed, make your way under a shady tree with a book and some snacks, people watch at a cafe, watch people on your electronic devices on your preferred streaming platform— you'll be pleasantly surprised by the international offerings—, work on crafting your travel journal, or absolutely nothing at all. Did I say that already? Remember that just by being on the trip you are already "making it count" there's no need to stress about "making up" for your recharge days. Self-care doesn't stop when you're traveling.

A glimpse of my favorite city in the world.
Taichung, Taiwan
August 2018

Houtanjing Sky Bridge in Changhua/Nantou
June 2019

## ABOUT THE AUTHOR

After a Fulbright scholarship in Taiwan lured by the intoxicating alchemy of unfamiliar territory, Brittany Edwards returned to the United States with her International Relations and Asian Studies double majors from Rollins College to continue her love for writing and creating. Her fascination with the intersection of linguistics and physics mirrors her love for challenging normative perspectives and merging disparate cultural identities. She is a well-rounded creative consultant and education lover who transfers seamlessly across industries and keeps social emotional learning at the heart of her philosophy, bringing more patience and compassion to interactions with anyone she meets.

_____

SIGNATURE OF AUTHOR

## TRAVELING BLACK WOMEN

**PASSPORT**

| TYPE | CODE OF ISSUER | PASSPORT NO. |
|---|---|---|
| P | TBW | AB1234567 |

SURNAME
EDWARDS

NAME
BRITTANY

IDENTIFICATION NO.
98765432M000AB987

NATIONALITY
JAMERICAN

PLACE OF HEART
TAIWAN

DATE OF TRIP
08 01 2018

AUTHORITY
TRAVELING BLACK WOMEN

P<TBWEDWARDS<<BRITTANY<<<<<<<<<<<<<<<<<<<<<<<<
AB12345670TBW0001020309876543 2M000AB987

## @_brittany_edwards_

_Follow her YouTube page (Brittany Edwards) where she shares her resourceful ways to tackle creative challenges and shares the detail of her days. Read her articles on the Medium platform & Black Asia Magazine._

www.travelingblackwomen.com

www.ingramcontent.com/pod-product-compliance
Lightning Source LLC
Chambersburg PA
CBHW040855120626
46551CB00001B/25